The Path to Harmony:
Spiritual Sanity for Parents and Business Owners

Bitrus Raphael Medugu

ISBN: 9798867667337

DEDICATION

This book is dedicated of Mr. Amos R. Medugu and to all struggling parents who are caught up between business and parenting.

CONTENTS

PREFACE

The Path to Harmony: Spiritual Sanity for Parents and Business Owners addresses the challenges faced by individuals juggling the demanding roles of parenthood and business ownership. This book advocates for the pursuit of spiritual sanity as a means to find balance and harmony in the midst of these responsibilities. It emphasizes the importance of embracing a spiritual mindset to navigate the complexities of both personal and professional life, promoting a fulfilling and purpose-driven existence.

The book explores the common struggles experienced by parents and business owners, emphasizing the potential neglect of spiritual well-being in the pursuit of success. It advocates for a broader definition of spirituality, encompassing a connection to something greater than oneself. Various practices such as self-reflection, mindfulness, and meditation are presented as tools to tap into this spiritual essence, providing strength and solace.

Benefits of prioritizing spiritual well-being are discussed, including the foundation it provides for conscious decision-making aligned with one's values, enhanced emotional well-being, and the cultivation of resilience to manage stress. The subchapter on achieving spiritual sanity offers practical tools and techniques tailored to the unique needs of parents and business owners, including strategies for time management, setting boundaries, and self-care rituals.

Conclusion: Embracing the Journey of Spiritual Sanity:
The conclusion reinforces the necessity for parents and business owners to prioritize their spiritual well-being amid the challenges of modern life. It highlights the impact of spiritual sanity on parenting, creating a harmonious environment for children to thrive. Similarly, in the realm of business ownership, aligning values with professional endeavors is emphasized for positive impact on employees, customers, and the world.

The journey of spiritual sanity is portrayed as an ongoing process requiring dedication, self-awareness, and a willingness to let go of control. The importance of openness to new perspectives, exploration of diverse spiritual practices, and seeking support is underscored. The conclusion invites readers to embark on this transformative journey, promoting a life of balance, joy, and purpose, and encouraging the inspiration of others.

The Path to Harmony: Spiritual Sanity for Parents and Business Owners serves as a guide for individuals seeking a harmonious existence amidst the challenges of dual responsibilities. Through self-reflection, practical tools, and a commitment to spiritual well-being, readers are encouraged to create environments that nurture personal growth, strong relationships, and professional success. The transformative power of spiritual sanity is presented as a key to unlocking fulfillment and peace within oneself, inspiring positive change in both personal and professional spheres.

INTRODUCTION

Are you a parent and a business owner who is struggling like the fiddler on the roof to maintain some Spiritual Sanity and balance? Well, here is good news for you. Here comes a path to harmony which I feel is a must read if you fall into this category. Although parenting and business are not mutually exclusive, yet the need for a meaningful balance between the two is inevitable for a productive harmony. It is in the light of this needed harmony that The Path to Harmony: Spiritual Sanity for Parents and Business Owners is here. This section will explore the invaluable journey towards achieving spiritual sanity for individuals who are both parents and business owners. By embracing a spiritual mindset, we can find balance and harmony in our personal and professional lives, ultimately leading to a more fulfilling and purpose-driven existence for our good and those of our families.

Parenting and running a business are two demanding roles that often leave individuals feeling overwhelmed and disconnected from their true selves as they appear to be caught up between two extremes. The pursuit of success in both areas can easily lead to neglecting our spiritual well-being. However, by recognizing the significance of spiritual sanity, we can learn to navigate these challenges while maintaining a sense of harmony in our lives.

Spirituality is not limited to religious practices; it encompasses a broader sense of connection to something greater than ourselves. By exploring our inner selves, connecting with nature, practicing mindfulness, or engaging in prayer and meditation, we can tap into our spiritual essence. This connection allows us to find solace, inner peace, and the strength needed to navigate the complexities of parenthood and business ownership.

When we prioritize our spiritual well-being, we unlock numerous benefits that positively impact our lives as parents and business owners. Spirituality provides us with a strong foundation, guiding us to make conscious decisions that align with our values and beliefs. It helps us cultivate resilience, manage stress, and enhance our emotional well-being. By embracing spiritual sanity, we create an environment that fosters personal growth, strong relationships, and professional success.

To achieve spiritual sanity, this subchapter provides practical tools and techniques tailored to the unique needs of parents and business owners. We explore strategies for time management, setting boundaries, and self-care rituals that nourish the mind, body, and soul. Additionally, we delve into the importance of cultivating a supportive community, seeking guidance from mentors, and integrating spiritual practices into our daily routines.

The Path to Harmony: Spiritual Sanity for Parents and Business Owners offers a transformative journey towards achieving spiritual sanity amidst the challenges of parenthood and business ownership. By embracing spirituality, we can find balance, purpose, and fulfillment in both areas of our lives. Through self- reflection and the application of practical tools and techniques, we can create a harmonious existence that nurtures our well-being, strengthens our connections, and propels us towards personal and professional success. Embark on this path today and discover the transformative power of spiritual sanity

CHAPTER 1: UNDERSTANDING THE CHALLENGES

In the ever-evolving tapestry of contemporary life, the first chapter, *Understanding the Challenges*, serves as an illuminating prologue to the nuanced landscape faced by those straddling the roles of both parents and business owners. As we navigate through the swift currents of this fast-paced world, a distinctive set of challenges unfolds before individuals shouldering the responsibilities of raising a family while steering the helm of entrepreneurial ventures.

It embarks on an exploration into what can be aptly described as 'The Modern Dilemma: Balancing Parenting and Business Ownership'. The intricacies of running a successful business and nurturing a family converge, creating a delicate dance that often leaves individuals feeling torn between their professional aspirations and personal obligations. As we delve into this multifaceted dilemma, the question echoing through these pages becomes poignant: How can one discover harmony and equilibrium amid the cacophony of competing priorities?

The Path to Harmony: Spiritual Sanity for Parents and Business Owners emerges as a guiding manual, offering not only valuable insights but also pragmatic strategies for navigating this delicate balance. The focal point of this exploration, encapsulated in the subchapter titled 'The Modern Dilemma: Balancing Parenting and Business Ownership', delves into the challenges unique to parents who also bear the mantle of business ownership. Here, the narrative unfolds to reveal how the concept of spiritual sanity provides a robust framework, a steady anchor amidst the tumult, facilitating the discovery of peace and fulfillment.

A crucial dimension of this delicate equilibrium lies in the realm of self-reflection. By taking the time to assess one's values and priorities, individuals can gain a profound clarity that guides them in making intentional decisions. This self-awareness becomes the compass, aligning actions with core beliefs, steering clear of the pitfalls of overwhelm and burnout.

The importance of setting boundaries takes center stage as another integral component of balancing the responsibilities of parenting and business ownership. Clear delineations between work and family time become imperative, ensuring that each facet of life receives the attention it deserves. By creating dedicated spaces for both business and family, individuals can better compartmentalize their roles, fostering a more meaningful presence in each area.

This subchapter delves further into the concept of self-care, a crucial aspect often neglected in the fervor of meeting the needs of others. Prioritizing practices such as exercise, meditation, and leisure activities become not just a luxury but a fundamental necessity for maintaining physical, mental, and spiritual well-being.

In the tapestry of this chapter, woven with threads of mindful and holistic approaches, spiritual sanity emerges as the linchpin. By embracing this spiritual perspective, individuals can navigate the modern dilemma with grace and intention. The subchapter acts as a guiding compass, offering a wealth of insights and practical advice to assist parents and business owners in finding the balance they seek, leading to a more fulfilling and harmonious life.

1.1 The Modern Dilemma: Balancing Parenting and Business Ownership

In today's fast-paced world, parents who are also business owners face a unique set of challenges. The demands of running a successful business and raising a family can often feel overwhelming, leaving many individuals feeling torn between their professional and personal responsibilities. This modern dilemma raises an important question: how can we find harmony and balance in the midst of these competing priorities?

The Path to Harmony: Spiritual Sanity for Parents and Business Owners is a guidebook that offers valuable insights and practical strategies for navigating this delicate balance. This subchapter, titled 'The Modern Dilemma: Balancing Parenting and Business Ownership,' delves deep into the challenges faced by parents who also double as business owners and explores how spiritual sanity can provide a framework for finding peace and fulfillment.

One of the key aspects of finding this balance is self-reflection. By taking the time to assess your values and priorities, you can gain clarity on what truly matters to you. This allows you to make conscious decisions that align with your core beliefs, both in your role as a parent and as a business owner. By being intentional in your choices, you can avoid the pitfalls of overwhelm and burnout.

Another important component of balancing parenting and business ownership is setting boundaries. It's crucial to establish clear boundaries between work and family time, ensuring that each aspect of your life receives the attention it deserves. By creating dedicated spaces for both your business and your family, you can better compartmentalize your responsibilities and be fully present in each area of your life when needed.

Additionally, this subchapter delves into the concept of self-care. As a parent and business owner, it's easy to neglect your own well-being in favor of meeting the needs of others. However, self-care is essential for maintaining your physical, mental, and spiritual health. By prioritizing self-care practices such as exercise, meditation, and leisure activities, you can replenish your energy and better serve both your family and your business.

Ultimately, finding harmony between parenting and business ownership requires a mindful and holistic approach. By embracing spiritual sanity, you can navigate the modern dilemma with grace and intention. This subchapter serves as a guide, offering insights and practical advice to help parents and business owners find the balance they seek, leading to a more fulfilling and harmonious life.

1.2 The Importance of Spiritual Sanity in Managing Responsibilities

Juggling the responsibilities of being a parent and a business owner can often leave one feeling overwhelmed and mentally exhausted in today's fast changing and demanding world. The constant pressure to succeed in both these roles can take a toll on our mental and emotional well-being. This is where the importance of spiritual sanity comes into play.

Spiritual sanity refers to the state of peace, clarity, and balance that can be achieved through nurturing our spiritual selves. It is the ability to find solace and strength amidst the chaos of our daily lives, allowing us to manage our responsibilities with grace and ease.

For parents and business owners, cultivating spiritual sanity is not just a luxury, but a necessity. It provides the much-needed foundation to navigate the challenges that come our way and make sound decisions for ourselves, our families, and our businesses.

One of the key benefits of spiritual sanity is the ability to maintain perspective. When we are caught up in the hustle and bustle of our responsibilities, it's easy to lose sight of what truly matters. Spiritual sanity allows us to step back, reflect, and prioritize our actions based on our core values and beliefs. It helps us align our actions with our higher purpose, ensuring that we are not just going through the motions but living a life of meaning and fulfillment.

Managing responsibilities can often lead to stress and anxiety. Spiritual sanity provides us with powerful tools to manage these emotions. Through practices such as meditation, mindfulness, and prayer, we can cultivate a sense of inner peace and tranquility. This, in turn, allows us to approach our responsibilities with a clear and calm mind, making better decisions and fostering healthier relationships with our children, partners, and employees.

Furthermore, spiritual sanity strengthens our resilience. It equips us with the ability to bounce back from setbacks and challenges that may arise in our personal and professional lives. By nurturing our spiritual selves, we tap into a source of inner strength and wisdom that helps us persevere in the face of adversity.

In conclusion, spiritual sanity is not a luxury but a vital aspect of managing responsibilities as parents and business owners. It provides us with the tools to maintain perspective, manage stress, and cultivate resilience. By investing time and effort into nurturing our spiritual selves, we can create a harmonious balance between our personal and professional lives, leading to a more fulfilling and successful journey.

1.3 Discovering and Facing the Challenges

In the journey of life, both as parents and business owners, we often encounter numerous challenges that test our resilience, patience, and inner strength. These challenges come in various forms, from personal setbacks to professional obstacles, all of which can have a profound impact on our spiritual sanity. It is during these moments that we must discover and face these challenges head-on, in order to find harmony and maintain our spiritual well-being.

Discovering the challenges is an essential step towards finding inner peace and spiritual sanity. It involves introspection, self-reflection and acknowledging the areas in our lives that need attention. As parents, we may face difficulties in balancing our responsibilities towards our children and maintaining a healthy work-life balance. Business owners, on the other hand, may grapple with financial pressures, employee management, and the constant need to adapt to a rapidly changing market.

Once we have identified the challenges, the next step is to face them with courage and determination. Facing the challenges requires a mindset shift and a willingness to embrace discomfort. It may involve seeking guidance from mentors, therapists, or spiritual leaders who can provide valuable insights and guidance. It also necessitates developing resilience and the ability to bounce back from setbacks, understanding that challenges are an inherent part of growth and progress.

In the face of challenges, it is crucial to maintain our spiritual sanity. This means staying connected to our inner selves, our values, and our spiritual beliefs. Regular spiritual practices such as meditation, prayer, or mindfulness can provide solace and clarity during difficult times. Engaging in activities that bring us joy and fulfillment, such as spending quality time with loved ones or pursuing hobbies, can also help restore balance and perspective.

Furthermore, it is important to remember that challenges are not insurmountable obstacles but rather opportunities for growth. They provide us with valuable lessons, teach us resilience, and help us discover our true potential. By embracing challenges and viewing them as stepping stones towards personal and professional growth, we can navigate through them with grace and emerge stronger and wiser.

In conclusion, discovering and facing the challenges is an integral part of the path to spiritual sanity for parents and business owners. By acknowledging and addressing these challenges, we are able to find harmony and maintain our spiritual well-being. Through introspection, resilience, and connecting with our inner selves, we can transform challenges into opportunities for growth and personal development. Remember, the path to harmony lies in our ability to face challenges with courage, embrace discomfort, and emerge stronger on the other

CHAPTER 2: CULTIVATING INNER PEACE

In the relentless whirlwind of modern life, this chapter beckons you to explore the transformative journey of finding stillness in a busy world. Navigating the demands of parenting and business ownership, this chapter serves as a guide through the labyrinth of chaos, revealing a path to inner calm and spiritual sanity.

The very beginning addresses the common predicament faced by parents and business owners—an overwhelming sense of chaos and disconnection from one's true self in the face of relentless demands. Drawing from the expertise of renowned experts in the field of well-being and mindfulness. It emphasizes that within this chaos lies an accessible path to discovering inner calm.

Experts such as Dr. Jon Kabat-Zinn, a pioneer in the field of mindfulness, underscore the importance of finding stillness in the midst of chaos. His research and teachings have laid the groundwork for understanding how mindfulness practices can bring about a profound sense of tranquillity, even in the busiest of lives. As we embark on this exploration, the chapter delves into practical strategies and techniques inspired by Kabat-Zinn's work, offering readers a tangible approach to carve out moments of tranquillity amidst the hustle and bustle of life.

Recognizing the distinctive challenges faced by parents and business owners, the chapter unfolds into the exploration of the benefits of finding stillness. The narrative draws inspiration from the work of Dr. Shefali Tsabary, a clinical psychologist and author specializing in conscious parenting. Dr. Tsabary's insights underscore the ease with which parents can neglect their well-being, leading to burnout and a sense of emptiness. Through her lens, the chapter delves into the ways in which finding stillness nurtures spiritual sanity, enabling parents to become better nurturers and role models for their children.

Similarly, insights from business experts like Arianna Huffington, founder of Thrive Global, contribute to the understanding of the pressure faced by business owners. Huffington's emphasis on well-being and the connection between inner peace and professional success becomes a guiding principle. The subchapter introduces the concept of 'active stillness,' a state of inner calm inspired by Huffington's teachings, demonstrating how integrating moments of stillness into the workday enhances productivity and decision-making.

As the exploration deepens, the chapter introduces the concept of spiritual sanity—a notion resonating with the teachings of spiritual leaders such as Thich Nhat Hanh. Hanh's philosophy, rooted in mindfulness and connecting with something greater than oneself, becomes a cornerstone. The chapter explores various spiritual practices inspired by Hanh's teachings, such as gratitude journaling and connecting with nature, offering a holistic approach to restoring purpose and meaning in both personal and professional spheres.

The narrative consistently emphasizes that discovering stillness in a busy world is not a luxury but a necessity for well-being and sanity. Drawing from the collective wisdom of these experts, the chapter guides readers on a journey to prioritize moments of tranquillity, creating a harmonious and fulfilling life for both parents and business owners.

In the subsequent sections, the chapter unfolds into practical applications of mindfulness practices, drawing from the expertise of renowned mindfulness practitioners, and offers practical ways to nurture spiritual sanity. By incorporating tips inspired by experts such as Dr. Kabat-Zinn, Dr. Tsabary, and Arianna Huffington, the chapter provides actionable insights for individuals seeking balance amidst the demanding roles of parenthood and business ownership.

2.1 Finding Stillness in a Busy World

Finding stillness in our fast-paced and chaotic world can seem like an impossible task. As parents and business owners, the demands on our time and energy can leave us feeling overwhelmed and disconnected from our true selves. However, amidst the chaos, there is a path to discovering inner calm and spiritual sanity.

In this subchapter, we will explore the importance of finding stillness in a busy world and how it can benefit both parents and business owners. We will delve into practical strategies and techniques that can help you carve out moments of tranquillity amidst the hustle and bustle of everyday life.

As parents, it is easy to get caught up in the never-ending cycle of responsibilities, from managing the household to attending to the needs of our children. We often neglect our own well-being in the process, leading to burnout and a sense of emptiness. By finding stillness, we can nurture our own spiritual sanity, allowing us to show up as better parents and role models for our children. We will explore simple mindfulness exercises and meditation techniques that can be incorporated into even the busiest of schedules.

Similarly, as business owners, the pressure to constantly be on the go and achieve success can be overwhelming. However, locating stillness can actually enhance our productivity and decision-making abilities. We will discuss the concept of 'active stillness' – a state of inner calm that allows for greater clarity and focus. By incorporating moments of stillness into our workday, we can cultivate a more balanced and harmonious approach to business, ultimately leading to greater success and fulfillment.

We will also touch upon the concept of spiritual sanity – the idea that true fulfillment comes from aligning our actions with our values and connecting with something greater than ourselves. We will explore various spiritual practices, such as gratitude journaling and connecting with nature, that can help restore a sense of purpose and meaning in both our personal and professional lives.

As already noted, discovering stillness in a busy world is not a luxury but a necessity for our wellbeing and sanity. By prioritizing moments of tranquillity, we can create a more harmonious and fulfilling life as parents and business owners. Let us embark on this journey so you can reconnect with your inner self and discover the path to spiritual sanity amidst the chaos of modern life.

2.2 Mindfulness Practices for Parents and Business Owners

In today's busy world of parenting and running a business, finding a sense of inner peace and spiritual sanity can often feel like an elusive goal. The constant juggling of responsibilities, the pressure to succeed, and the never-ending demands can leave even the most resilient individuals feeling overwhelmed and disconnected. However, by incorporating mindfulness practices into your daily routine, you can cultivate a deeper sense of harmony and spiritual well-being.

The following tips that can assist parents and business owners to attain some balance.

1. ***Start your day with intention***: Before jumping into the chaos of the day, take a few moments to set an intention for how you want to show up as a parent and business owner. Reflect on your values and goals and visualize yourself navigating the challenges with grace and mindfulness.

2. ***Practice gratitude***: Throughout the day, take moments to express gratitude for the blessings in your life. Whether it's a simple appreciation for your child's laughter or gratitude for a successful

business deal, cultivating an attitude of gratitude can shift your focus from stress to abundance.

3. *Mindful breathing*: Whenever you find yourself feeling overwhelmed or stressed, take a pause and focus on your breath. Close your eyes, take deep breaths in and out, and allow yourself to fully experience the present moment. This simple practice can help you regain clarity and composure.

4. *Set boundaries*: As a parent and business owner, it's crucial to establish boundaries to protect your well-being. Learn to say 'no' when necessary, delegate tasks, and create designated time for self-care and family. By setting clear boundaries, you can maintain a healthy work-life balance and prevent burnout.

5.*Mindful communication*: In both parenting and business, effective communication is vital. Practice active listening, speak with intention, and approach conversations with empathy and compassion. By being fully present in your interactions, you can foster stronger connections and resolve conflicts more effectively.

6. *Embrace imperfection*: As parents and business owners, we often strive for perfection. However, embracing imperfection is essential for maintaining spiritual sanity. Give yourself permission to make mistakes, learn from them, and let go of unrealistic expectations. Remember that growth and progress often come from embracing imperfection.

By incorporating these mindfulness practices into your daily life, you can cultivate a deeper sense of spiritual sanity as a parent and business owner. Remember, the path to harmony is not about achieving perfection but rather finding balance, peace, and inner well-being amidst life's challenges. Embrace the journey and allow mindfulness to guide you towards a more fulfilling and harmonious life.

2.3 Practical ways of Nurture Spiritual Sanity

Here are some practical ways to cultivate spiritual sanity amidst the demanding roles of being a parent and a business owner. It is no secret that juggling these responsibilities can be overwhelming, often leaving us feeling disconnected from our inner selves and the larger spiritual realm. However, by integrating simple yet effective practices into our daily lives, we can find a path to harmony and rediscover our spiritual well-being.

➢ ***Mindful Breathing***: Begin each day with a few moments of deep, conscious breathing. This practice helps center your mind, calm your nervous system, and create a space for spiritual connection. Throughout the day, take regular breaks to focus on your breath, allowing yourself to recharge and find clarity amidst the chaos.

➢ ***Gratitude Journaling***: Cultivate an attitude of gratitude by maintaining a gratitude journal. Each day, write down at least three things you are grateful for, be it the love and support of your family or the success of your business. This practice shifts your focus towards the positive aspects of your life, fostering a sense of contentment and spiritual well-being.

➢ ***Setting Intentions***: Start your workday or family time with intention. Take a few moments to set clear, positive intentions for your day, such as being present in your interactions, making conscious decisions, or finding joy in the small moments. By setting intentions, you align your actions with your higher purpose, infusing them with spiritual significance.

➢ ***Mindful Parenting***: Incorporate mindfulness into your parenting journey. Be fully present with your children, actively listening to them without distractions. Engage in activities that promote connection, such as family meals or nature walks. By being mindful parents, we create a sacred space for our children to grow spiritually and emotionally.

➢ **Seeking Support**: Surround yourself with a supportive community of like-minded individuals who understand the challenges of balancing parenthood and business ownership. Engage in spiritual forums, join local groups, or seek a mentor who can guide you on your path to spiritual sanity.

➢ *Self-Care Rituals*: Prioritize self-care to replenish your spiritual reservoir. Engage in activities that nourish your mind, body, and soul, such as meditation, yoga, reading, or spending time in nature. By taking care of yourself, you ensure you have the energy and clarity to fulfill your roles as a parent and business owner.

By implementing these practical ways into your daily life, you can begin to restore spiritual sanity and find harmony amidst the demanding roles of being a parent and a business owner. Remember, it is through nurturing our own spiritual well-being that we can create a positive, enriching environment for our families and businesses.

CHAPTER 3: NURTURING THE SELF

Considering the dynamic landscape of modern responsibilities, this chapter unfolds as a crucial guide for parents and business owners, emphasizing the paramount importance of self-care. It draws insights from experts in well-being, business management, and spirituality to offer practical strategies for achieving spiritual sanity while balancing the intricate demands of parenthood and business ownership.

As the chapter commences, it navigates through the complexities faced by parents and business owners in the 21st century. Acknowledging the challenges, the subchapter leans on the wisdom of renowned psychologist and boundary-setting expert, Dr. Henry Cloud. Dr. Cloud's work becomes a cornerstone for the exploration of the necessity of establishing clear boundaries between work and family life. It delves into specific working hours and the dedication to quality family time, referencing Dr. Cloud's expertise to underline the importance of being fully present in both realms. The Chapter further incorporates mindfulness practices inspired by the teachings of mindfulness expert Dr. Ellen Langer. By infusing mindfulness into daily routines through activities like meditation and self-reflection, the narrative aligns with Dr. Langer's emphasis on achieving a calmer and more focused mindset to navigate the challenges of parenting and business ownership. It lays emphasis on prioritizing mental and emotional well-being. Drawing from the expertise of Dr. Dan Siegel, a clinical professor and proponent of interpersonal neurobiology, the narrative emphasizes the intersection of spiritual sanity and brain health. Dr. Siegel's insights shape the exploration of strategies such as mindfulness techniques, stress management tools, and self-care practices that contribute to nurturing mental and emotional well-being.

The narrative incorporates the relational expertise of Dr. John Gottman, a renowned psychologist specializing in marital stability and emotional well-being. By highlighting the importance of fostering healthy relationships and effective communication, the chapter encourages parents and business owners to create supportive networks, seek guidance, and nurture connections for overall well-being. The chapter concludes by delving into the indispensable role of rest in maintaining spiritual sanity. Drawing inspiration from Lao Tzu's timeless wisdom, the narrative underscores the importance of taking time to rest in a world that often glorifies perpetual productivity. The discussion aligns with the insights of Dr. Matthew Walker, a sleep scientist, emphasizing the restorative power of adequate sleep for physical, mental, and spiritual well-being.

In the grand tapestry of achieving spiritual sanity, this chapter serves as a beacon, weaving together the wisdom of experts such as Dr. Henry Cloud, Dr. Ellen Langer, Dr. Dan Siegel, Dr. John Gottman, and Lao Tzu, offering a roadmap for parents and business owners to prioritize self-care, mental and emotional well-being, and the essential practice of taking time to rest. As we embark on this journey, let us heed the collective wisdom of these experts to cultivate a harmonious and fulfilling life in the midst of our multifaceted responsibilities.

3.1 Self-Care Strategies for Parents and Business Owners

In the 21st century, administering the responsibilities of parenthood and running a business can be mind-boggling. It is crucial to prioritize self-care to maintain our overall well-being and achieve spiritual sanity. In this regard, below are some valuable strategies and techniques that can help you strike a balance between your personal and professional life.

1. *Set Boundaries*: It's essential to establish clear boundaries between work and family life. Sey specific working hours and dedicate quality time to your family, free from any work-related

distractions. This will ensure that you are fully present in both aspects of your life.

2. *Practice Mindfulness*: Incorporate mindfulness techniques into your daily routine. Take a few moments each day to engage in activities that promote inner peace and self-reflection. This may include meditation, deep breathing exercises, or simply taking a walk-in nature. Mindfulness will help you navigate the challenges of parenting and business ownership with a calmer and more focused mind.

3. *Delegate and Outsource*: As a business owner and parent, it's crucial to understand that you can't do it all. Delegate tasks and responsibilities to trusted employees or family members. Consider outsourcing certain aspects of your business to lighten your workload. By doing so, you will free up more time for self-care and reduce the stress associated with trying to handle everything on your own.

4. *Prioritize Self-Care Activities*: Make self-care a non-negotiable part of your routine. Engage in activities that bring you joy and relaxation, such as reading, exercising, pursuing hobbies, or spending quality time with loved ones. By prioritizing self-care, you will replenish your energy and be better equipped to handle the demands of both parenthood and business ownership.

5. *Seek Support*: Don't hesitate to reach out for help when needed. Surround yourself with a supportive network of friends, family members, or fellow business owners who understand your unique challenges. Joining parenting or business owner groups can provide invaluable support, advice, and a sense of community.

Remember, taking care of yourself is not selfish; it is a necessity for maintaining your spiritual sanity as a parent and business owner. By implementing these self-care strategies into your life, you will find yourself better equipped to navigate the journey towards harmony and achieve success in both your personal and professional endeavours.

3.2 Prioritizing Mental and Emotional Well-being

The importance of mental and emotional well-being cannot be overemphasized. It is sacrosanct that parents and business owners make this reality a priority. To help achieve this, this part of the work addresses the significance of spiritual sanity in achieving a harmonious life, offering valuable insights and practical advice for those navigating the dual roles of parenting and managing a business.

As parents, we often find ourselves managing numerous responsibilities, feeling sometimes crushed by the constant demands of our children and the pressures of our careers. Similarly, business owners face the incessant challenges of managing employees, meeting targets, and maintaining a competitive edge. In such a frenetic environment, it is all too easy to neglect our own mental and emotional well-being, leading to burnout, stress, and an overall sense of dissatisfaction.

However, by prioritizing our spiritual sanity, we can regain balance and find inner peace amidst the chaos. This involves cultivating practices that nourish our minds, bodies, and souls, enabling us to tackle our responsibilities with clarity, compassion, and resilience.

There are various strategies to enhance mental and emotional well-being, including mindfulness techniques, stress management tools, and self-care practices. For example, the importance of carving out quality time to recreate, whether through meditation, exercise, or engaging in hobbies that bring us joy and fulfillment. By taking care of our own needs, we become better equipped to meet the needs of our children and our businesses.

Furthermore, spiritual sanity involves fostering healthy relationships and effective communication. Surrounding ourselves with a supportive network, seeking guidance and mentorship, and nurturing connections both at home and in the workplace is of great importance. By building strong relationships, we create a foundation of trust, collaboration, and understanding, which contributes to our overall well-being and success.

Ultimately, prioritizing our mental and emotional well-being as parents and business owners allows us to lead more fulfilling lives. It enables us to approach challenges with grace, make sound decisions, and create a harmonious environment for ourselves, our families, and our businesses. By investing in our spiritual sanity, we enhance our capacity to thrive in all areas of life, experiencing a sense of peace, purpose, and joy.

3.3 Taking Time to Rest

The place of rest in our spiritual sanity cannot be over-emphasized. In fact, it is as inevitable to the life of our spiritual well-being as breathing is, to the life of the body. Given the busy nature of our world today, parents and business owners often find themselves caught in a never-ending cycle of productivity and responsibility. The demands of managing a family and running a business can take a toll on one's physical, mental, and spiritual well-being. However, it is crucial for both parents and business owners to recognize the importance of taking time to rest in order to maintain spiritual sanity.

Resting is not a sign of weakness or laziness; it is a necessary part of achieving balance and harmony in life. When we neglect to rest, we become susceptible to burnout, stress, and a decline in our overall well-being. As parents and business owners, we have a responsibility not only to ourselves but also to our families and employees. By taking time to rest, we are better equipped to fulfill these responsibilities with clarity, focus, and a renewed sense of purpose.

Resting can take many forms, depending on individual preferences and circumstances. It could involve taking a vacation, spending quality time with loved ones, engaging in a hobby or creative pursuit, or simply taking a day off to relax and recharge. The key is to disconnect from the demands of work and allow us to rejuvenate both mentally and spiritually.

Resting also provides an opportunity for introspection and self-reflection. It allows us to step back from the daily grind and gain perspective on our lives and priorities. By creating space for silence and solitude, we can tap into our inner wisdom and access a deeper level of spiritual sanity. This, in turn, enables us to make better decisions, cultivate healthy relationships, and foster a sense of connection with something greater than ourselves.

In a world that glorifies busyness and productivity, taking time to rest may feel like a luxury. However, it is essential for maintaining our spiritual sanity as parents and business owners. By prioritizing rest, we are not only investing in our own well-being but also setting an example for our children and employees. We are teaching them the value of self-care, balance, and the importance of nourishing the soul.

In conclusion, taking time to rest is a vital component of achieving spiritual sanity for parents and business owners. It allows us to recharge, gain perspective, and connect with our inner selves. By prioritizing rest, we can create a harmonious and fulfilling life that extends beyond the realms of work and responsibility. Let us remember the wisdom in the words of Lao Tzu: "Nature does not hurry, yet everything is accomplished."

CHAPTER 4: BUILDING HEALTHY RELATIONSHIPS

This chapter offers a profound exploration into achieving harmony through spiritual sanity while navigating the intricate dance of balancing family and work. Drawing inspiration from the foundational work of Dr. Henry Cloud on setting boundaries, it unveils the crucial role of clear demarcations between work and family life. This, combined with the practical time management strategies advocated by renowned organizational psychologist Dr. Stephen R. Covey, forms a blueprint for parents and business owners to efficiently navigate their dual roles without succumbing to overwhelming stress. It further underscores the importance of nurturing one's spirituality, echoing the insights of Dr. Wayne Dyer, as a means to find equilibrium amidst the challenges of balancing family and work dynamics.

In a world characterized by constant change, the linchpin of harmonious relationships for parents and business owners— effective communication is brought to bear. Rooted in the wisdom of Dr. John Gottman, a pioneer in marital stability, this chapter introduces communication as the bedrock for healthy parent-child relationships. It integrates practical tips from his research on active listening, emphasizing the significance of understanding and respecting boundaries. Transitioning into the business realm, the chapter taps into the insights of Dr. Marshall B. Rosenberg, the founder of Nonviolent Communication, shedding light on transparent and efficient communication within organizations. By intertwining these principles with the spiritual sanity paradigm, the chapter guides individuals on a transformative journey, fostering connections based on empathy, understanding, and authenticity.

In conclusion the chapter illuminates the often-neglected realms of recreation and networking, crucial for restoring harmony and achieving spiritual sanity. It draws from the profound philosophy of

Lao Tzu and the rejuvenating aspects of recreation, emphasizing the insights of Dr. Stuart Brown, a pioneer in the study of play. The narrative seamlessly weaves the importance of leisure activities in reducing stress and nurturing spiritual well-being. Simultaneously, it incorporates the networking expertise of Dr. Ivan Misner, the founder of BNI, as a tool for personal and professional growth. The chapter articulates how recreation and networking, when harmonized, become essential components for parents and business owners on the path to spiritual sanity. Through the wisdom of these experts, the chapter unveils a transformative approach to building healthy relationships, enriching lives both personally and professionally.

4.1 Balancing Family and Work Dynamics

Maintaining a healthy balance between family and business is a herculean task today due to social demands. Those who double as parents and business owners are often caught up in this quagmire and they struggle to find a balance. The constant running act can take a toll on their overall well-being and lead to feelings of stress. However, achieving harmony in both areas is not an impossible feat. By embracing the concept of spiritual sanity, parents and business owners can find the balance they seek and create a fulfilling and harmonious life.

Spiritual sanity revolves around the idea of aligning one's inner values and beliefs with their external actions and choices. It emphasizes the importance of nurturing the mind, body, and spirit to create a sense of peace and contentment. When applied to the challenges of balancing family and work dynamics, it becomes a powerful tool for finding equilibrium and fulfillment.

One key aspect of achieving this balance is setting clear boundaries. As a business owner, it is crucial to establish dedicated work hours and stick to them. This allows for focused and efficient work, preventing it from encroaching on precious family time. Likewise, it is essential to designate specific family time and protect it sincerely from work-related distractions. By creating these boundaries, parents can ensure that both their business and family receive the attention they deserve.

Moreover, practicing effective time management is vital in maintaining balance. Learning to prioritize tasks and delegate responsibilities when necessary is crucial. It allows parents to focus on the most important aspects of their work and family life, without feeling overwhelmed by an ever-growing to-do list. By setting realistic goals and managing time efficiently, parents and business owners can create space for themselves and their loved ones.

In addition to practical strategies, nurturing one's spirituality is essential in finding harmony. Taking time for self-reflection, meditation, or engaging in activities that bring joy and peace can rejuvenate the mind, body, and spirit. Connecting with one's spirituality allows individuals to tap into their inner strength and wisdom, making it easier to navigate the challenges of balancing family and work dynamics.

Ultimately, achieving balance between family and work is an ongoing journey. It requires constant self-reflection, adjustment, and a commitment to spiritual sanity. By setting boundaries, managing time effectively, and nurturing one's spirituality, parents and business owners can create a harmonious life that brings fulfillment, happiness, and a sense of purpose. Embracing the path to harmony allows individuals to not only succeed in their business ventures but also create lasting and meaningful connections with their families.

4.2 Effective Communication for Harmonious Relationships

The Struggle to maintain a sense of balance and harmony for parents and business owners in our fast-changing world is by no means an easy-going optimism; the key to success in this regard lies in effective communication. Establishing harmonious relationships within the realms of both parenting and business can be a challenging task, but with the right tools and mindset, it is certainly achievable.

This section explores the importance of effective communication in fostering harmonious relationships, focusing on the specific niche of spiritual sanity. As parents and business owners, it is vital to recognize that communication is not solely about exchanging words but also about understanding, empathy, and connection.

In the realm of parenting, effective communication is essential for maintaining a healthy relationship with our children. By actively listening to their concerns and desires, we can create an environment of trust and open dialogue. The power of active listening, which offers practical tips and techniques to enhance communication with our children is also brought to bear. Furthermore, it emphasizes the significance of setting clear boundaries and expressing expectations effectively, fostering a harmonious parent-child relationship rooted in understanding and respect.

Within the context of business, effective communication is the backbone of successful collaborations and partnerships. This subchapter also explores the importance of transparent and efficient communication channels within an organization, highlighting the positive impact it has on employee satisfaction, productivity, and overall success. It also delves into the significance of active communication with clients, suppliers, and stakeholders, providing strategies to foster harmonious professional relationships.

Drawing from the niche of spiritual sanity, this section places emphasis on the importance of mindful communication. It encourages parents and business owners to engage in self-reflection and introspection, enabling them to communicate from a place of calmness and authenticity. By incorporating mindfulness techniques into their communication practices, individuals can enhance their ability to connect with others on a deeper level and build relationships based on mutual understanding and empathy.

Overall, effective communication serves as the cornerstone for building harmonious relationships in both parenting and business. Practical advice, strategies, and insights to help parents and business owners cultivate an environment of trust, understanding, and open dialogue is also discussed. By prioritizing effective communication, individuals can navigate the challenges of modern life, finding a path to harmony in their personal and professional relationships.

4.3 Recreation and Networking

More than ever, the demands of the daily lives of parents and business owners in the face of a challenging world could be so heavy a task to manage. Balancing the responsibilities of raising a family and running a successful business can be a daunting task, leaving little time for personal well-being and spiritual growth. However, by recognizing the importance of recreation and networking, we can begin to restore harmony and achieve spiritual sanity in our lives.

Recreation, often overlooked in our busy schedules, is essential for our overall well-being. It allows us to unwind, recharge, and reconnect with ourselves and our loved ones. Engaging in leisure activities that bring us joy and relaxation not only reduces stress but also nurtures our spiritual selves. Whether it's taking a walk in the wild, practicing yoga, or pursuing a hobby, recreation helps us to find balance and rejuvenation amidst life's chaos.

Moreover, recreation provides an opportunity for self-reflection and introspection. When we engage in activities that bring us joy, our minds become clear, and we are more receptive to the whispers of our inner selves. This newfound clarity not only enhances our decision-making skills but also allows us to tap into our spirituality, fostering a deeper sense of purpose and fulfillment.

Networking, on the other hand, is a powerful tool for personal and professional growth. As parents and business owners, connecting with like-minded individuals can provide valuable support, guidance, and inspiration. By attending conferences, joining industry- specific groups, or participating in online communities, we can expand our networks and surround ourselves with individuals who share our values and aspirations.

Networking also offers an opportunity for personal development, as it exposes us to different perspectives and ideas. By engaging in meaningful conversations, sharing experiences, and learning from others, we broaden our horizons and challenge our own beliefs. This exchange of knowledge and wisdom not only enriches our lives but also nurtures our spiritual sanity.

In conclusion, recreation and networking are vital components of achieving spiritual sanity as parents and business owners. By prioritizing time for leisure and engaging in activities that bring us joy, we can restore balance and nurture our spiritual selves. Additionally, by actively seeking connections and engaging in meaningful conversations with like-minded individuals, we expand our horizons and gain valuable support. Through the pursuit of recreation and networking, we can embark on the path to harmony and find spiritual sanity amidst the challenges of our daily lives.

CHAPTER 5: ALIGNING VALUES AND PURPOSE

Chapter five focuses on the fundamental importance of aligning personal and professional values to attain spiritual sanity. Rooted in the insights of Dr. Stephen R. Covey, renowned for his work on the role of values in effective living, the chapter elucidates the profound impact of defining personal values. It draws parallels between Covey's principles and the complexities of parenting, emphasizing the pivotal role of values as a moral compass. Similarly, Dr. Howard Gardner's work on ethical decision-making in professional settings serves as a guiding light for business owners striving to align actions with personal beliefs. By echoing Covey's call for self-reflection, this chapter empowers parents and business owners to navigate the nuanced process of defining values, ensuring a life of authenticity and purpose.

As parents and entrepreneurs grapple with the intricate dance between familial responsibilities and professional pursuits, this chapter further unfolds the transformative narrative of 'Aligning Passion and Purpose in Parenting and Business.' Rooted in the wisdom of Viktor Frankl, the father of logotherapy, the chapter underscores the profound connection between passion, purpose, and spiritual sanity. By aligning parenting passion with the purpose of nurturing compassionate and empowered individuals, individuals unlock the true potential of their roles as parents. Simultaneously, the chapter draws inspiration from the insights of Sir Richard Branson, epitomizing aligning passion and purpose in the business realm. It highlights the symbiotic relationship between spiritual sanity and purpose-driven entrepreneurship, urging individuals to infuse authenticity, empathy, and integrity into their professional endeavors. Through the amalgamation of these principles, the chapter sets the stage for a transformative journey toward true fulfillment and harmony.

In conclusion, it illuminates the path of spiritual sanity by exploring the art of 'Making the Right Decisions' for parents and business owners. Building on the wisdom of Dr. Wayne Dyer and the philosophy of mindfulness, the chapter demystifies the decision-making process. It advocates for self-awareness as championed by Dyer, emphasizing the importance of aligning decisions with core values for a sense of fulfillment. Echoing the mindfulness practices, it encourages consciousness in decision-making, a theme resonant with Jon Kabat-Zinn's teachings. By incorporating spiritual practices into the decision-making framework, the chapter, inspired by Kabat-Zinn's mindfulness-based stress reduction, unveils a transformative approach to navigate the complexities of parenting and business ownership. As parents and business owners embark on the journey of making decisions in alignment with their spiritual values, they pave the way for a harmonious and balanced life.

5.1 Defining Personal and Professional Values

Finding a sense of balance and harmony for parents and business owners is an essential part which leads to success especially in the chaotic world of today. This subchapter, while "Defining Personal and Professional Values," also explores the importance of understanding and aligning our personal and professional values to achieve spiritual sanity.

As parents, our values serve as a compass for navigating the challenges of raising children in a society that often pulls us in conflicting directions. By defining our personal values, we can create a solid moral foundation that will guide us in making decisions and setting priorities. Whether it is integrity, compassion, love, or respect, identifying and living by our values allows us to model these qualities for our children, fostering their growth into responsible and ethical individuals.

Similarly, business owners face unique challenges in maintaining spiritual sanity amidst the pressures of the corporate world. By defining our professional values, we can establish a framework for ethical decision-making, guiding our actions in a way that aligns with our personal beliefs. Whether it is transparency, innovation, or social responsibility, identifying our professional values helps us create a positive work environment that attracts like-minded individuals and nurtures their growth.

The process of defining personal and professional values begins with self-reflection. Taking the time to assess our core beliefs, desires, and aspirations allows us to gain clarity on what truly matters to us. It is crucial to distinguish between societal expectations and our true, authentic selves. By acknowledging our values, we can align our daily actions with our higher purpose, paving the way for a more fulfilling and meaningful life.

Once we have identified our personal and professional values, it is essential to integrate them into our daily lives. This requires consciously making choices that are in alignment with our values, even when faced with difficult decisions. By continuously evaluating our actions and their impact on ourselves, our families, and our businesses, we can ensure that we are living a life of integrity and purpose.

Conclusively, defining personal and professional values is a vital step towards achieving spiritual sanity for parents and business owners. By aligning our actions with our core beliefs, we create a sense of harmony and fulfillment in our lives. This subchapter aims to guide parents and business owners in the process of self-reflection and value identification, empowering them to create a life that is both spiritually and professionally rewarding.

5.2 Aligning Passion and Purpose in Parenting and Business

Although as parents and business owners, we often find ourselves caught up in the daily grind of diverse responsibilities and meeting the demands of both worlds, it is crucial to remember that our roles as parents and entrepreneurs are not mutually exclusive but rather intertwined. It is within this delicate balance that we can find true harmony and fulfillment.

This subchapter, "Aligning Passion and Purpose in Parenting and Business," explores the importance of nurturing our spiritual sanity to create a meaningful and purposeful life. By aligning our passions and purposes in both parenting and business, we can cultivate a sense of fulfillment that transcends the mundane and brings us closer to our true selves.

Parenting is an incredible journey that demands our utmost dedication and love. It is through this role that we learn the art of selflessness and discover the depth of our capacity for compassion and understanding. By aligning our passions and purpose in parenting, we can create an environment that fosters growth and nurtures our children's spirits. This entails being present, actively listening, and guiding them with love and respect. When we align our passion for parenting with our purpose to raise compassionate and empowered individuals, we unlock the true potential of our role as parents.

Similarly, as business owners, we have the opportunity to align our passion and purpose to create a positive impact. It is not just about making a profit but also about making a difference in the lives of others. When we align our passion for our business with our purpose to serve and uplift, we experience a deep sense of fulfillment. By nurturing our spiritual sanity, we can infuse our business practices with integrity, empathy, and authenticity, creating a harmonious and purpose-driven workplace.

Aligning passion and purpose in both parenting and business requires self-reflection, intentionality, and a commitment to personal growth. It is a continuous journey that evolves with time and experience. By cultivating our spiritual sanity, we can find the balance and alignment needed to navigate the challenges of parenting and entrepreneurship with grace and wisdom.

Emphasis also lain on the crucial role of spiritual sanity in the lives of parents and business owners. By aligning our passions and purposes in both realms, we can create a life of meaning, fulfillment, and harmony. It is through this alignment that we can truly make a difference in the world, whether it be through raising compassionate children or running purpose-driven businesses. Let us embark on this journey together, embracing the power of aligning passion and purpose in our lives.

5.3 Making the Right Decisions

Decision making could often be a daunting task for parents and business owners due to the pressure involved in such a combination. The constant runs of responsibilities, the pressures of meeting expectations, and the desire to find balance in both personal and professional life can leave parents and business owners feeling worn out and disconnected from their core values. However, by embracing the concept of spiritual sanity, one can navigate through life's challenges with clarity and confidence.

Spiritual sanity is not about religion or adhering to a specific belief system, but rather about finding inner peace and aligning with one's true self. It involves embracing mindfulness, self-reflection, and incorporating spiritual practices into daily life. By doing so, parents and business owners can gain a deeper understanding of themselves and their purpose, enabling them to make decisions that are in line with their values and bring about harmony in all aspects of life. Below are a few practical tips.

1. *Self-awareness*: One key aspect of making the right decisions is developing a strong sense of self-awareness. This involves taking the time to reflect on one's thoughts, emotions, and actions, and examining how they align with one's core values. By cultivating self-awareness, parents and business owners can make decisions that are rooted in authenticity and integrity, leading to a greater sense of fulfillment and peace.

2. *Practice Consciousness*: Another important factor in making the right decisions is practicing consciousness. This involves being fully present in the moment, without judgment or attachment to the past or future. By practicing consciousness, parents and business owners can approach decision-making with a clear and focused mind, free from distractions and anxieties. This allows for a more objective and balanced perspective, enabling them to make decisions that are in the best interest of all parties involved.

3. *Spiritual Practices*: Incorporating spiritual practices into daily life can provide guidance and support in decision-making. Whether it's through meditation, prayer, or engaging in acts of kindness and compassion, these practices can deepen one's connection to a higher power or inner wisdom. By tapping into this source of guidance, parents and business owners can make decisions that are in alignment with their spiritual values, bringing about a sense of peace and harmony.

In conclusion, making the right decisions in the context of parenting and business ownership requires a commitment to spiritual sanity. By cultivating self-awareness, practicing mindfulness, and incorporating spiritual practices into daily life, parents and business owners can navigate the complexities of decision-making with clarity and confidence. Embracing spiritual sanity not only brings about a greater sense of fulfillment and peace, but also allows for decisions that are in alignment with one's values, ultimately leading to a more harmonious and balanced life.

CHAPTER 6: EMBRACING CHANGE AND UNCERTAINTY

In the sometimes-conflicting demands of parenthood and business ownership, the pursuit of balance and spiritual sanity seems elusive amid the whirlwind of responsibilities and endless to-do lists. However, within the turbulence of transitions lies a hidden opportunity for growth and self-discovery. As parents and business owners grapple with inevitable life changes—be it the joyous arrival of a new family member, business expansion, or unexpected challenges—this chapter explores the crucial role of adaptation during these transformative times. Drawing from the insights of experts such as William Bridges, known for his work on managing transitions, and Susan Johnson, renowned for her expertise in relationship dynamics, the chapter underscores the significance of recognizing the delicate equilibrium between fulfilling parental and entrepreneurial responsibilities while nurturing one's spiritual well-being. By prioritizing self-care, fostering flexibility, and seeking community support, individuals can navigate transitions with grace, transforming them from daunting obstacles into opportunities for profound personal and professional development.

In the unpredictable world we navigate as parents and business owners, uncertainties have become an inevitable facet of our lives. This section delves into the challenges and pressures accompanying uncertainties, presenting a transformative perspective that encourages embracing uncertainty with grace and resilience. Drawing inspiration from experts such as Pema Chödrön, known for her teachings on navigating difficult times, and Rick Hanson, a neuroscientist exploring the intersection of brain science and contemplative practices, the chapter guides individuals toward cultivating spiritual sanity amid uncertain times. By developing trust, fostering resilience, and embracing mindfulness, this segment provides practical strategies to navigate uncertainties with poise. Through personal anecdotes, expert insights, and practical exercises, the transformative journey towards embracing uncertainty becomes a pathway to inner peace, balance, and fulfillment amidst the chaos of life's uncertainties.

Change, the constant companion in our journey through life, often leaves parents and business owners feeling overwhelmed and uncertain. This chapter advocates for finding the courage to not merely accept change but to embrace it as an opportunity for growth and transformation. Drawing on the wisdom of change management expert John P. Kotter and vulnerability researcher Brené Brown, the chapter explores the necessity of cultivating resilience, adaptability, and a deep connection to one's inner self. By acknowledging the inevitability of change in both parenting and business, individuals can create nurturing environments for their children's development and foster sustainable growth and success in their ventures. The transformative journey toward spiritual sanity amidst change involves self-reflection, mindfulness practices, and the continuous courage to navigate the unknown.

6.1 Adapting to Transitions as a Parent and Business Owner

It may appear to be an impossible task for parents and business owners to find balance and maintain spiritual sanity in today's world due to the pressure our roles impact. In fact, as parents and business owners, we often find ourselves so caught in a whirlwind of responsibilities, deadlines, and endless to-do lists that we wonder if we could ever find a way out. Well, here is the good news; it is in fact during times of transition that our ability to adapt becomes crucial.

Transitions are an inevitable part of life, whether it's welcoming a new addition to the family, expanding our business, or navigating through unexpected challenges. These moments can be both exciting and overwhelming, presenting us with unique opportunities for growth and self-discovery. Adapting to these transitions requires a delicate balance between fulfilling our responsibilities as parents and entrepreneurs while nurturing our spiritual well-being.

One of the key aspects of adapting to transitions is recognizing the importance of self-care. As parents and business owners, we often put the needs of others before our own, neglecting our physical, emotional, and spiritual health. However, in order to navigate through transitions successfully, we must prioritize self-care and make time for activities that replenish our energy and bring us joy. Whether it's practicing mindfulness, engaging in regular exercise, or spending quality time with loved ones, self-care is essential for maintaining spiritual sanity during times of change.

Another vital aspect of adapting to transitions is cultivating a mindset of flexibility and resilience. As parents and business owners, we must be willing to embrace change and adapt our plans accordingly. This requires letting go of rigid expectations and being open to new possibilities. By cultivating a mindset of flexibility, we can navigate through transitions with grace and ease, allowing us to find harmony between our roles as parents and entrepreneurs.

Furthermore, seeking support from a community of like-minded individuals can greatly enhance our ability to adapt to transitions. The journey of parenthood and entrepreneurship can be isolating at times, making it crucial to connect with others who understand our unique challenges and experiences. By joining support groups, attending workshops, or seeking guidance from mentors, we can find solace and inspiration during times of transition.

In conclusion, adapting to transitions as a parent and business owner requires a holistic approach that encompasses self-care flexibility, and community support. By prioritizing our physical, emotional, and spiritual well-being, embracing change with an open mind, and seeking support from others, we can navigate through transitions with grace and maintain spiritual sanity. Remember, transitions are not obstacles but opportunities for growth and self-discovery. Embrace them, and you will find harmony in the delicate dance of parenthood and entrepreneurship.

6.2 Embracing Uncertainty with Grace and Resilience

There is no doubt that uncertainties have become an inevitable part of our lives in our unpredictable world of today. As parents and business owners, we often find ourselves grappling with the challenges and pressures that come with these uncertainties. However, by embracing uncertainty with grace and resilience, we can navigate through these uncertain times and find a sense of spiritual sanity.

Uncertainty can trigger fear and anxiety, leading us to make hasty decisions or become paralyzed by indecisiveness. But what if we could shift our mindset and view uncertainty as an opportunity for growth and self-discovery? This section aims to guide parents and business owners towards embracing uncertainty with grace and resilience, cultivating spiritual sanity in the process.

One key aspect of embracing uncertainty is developing a sense of trust. Trusting in ourselves, in the greater forces at play, and in the journey we are embarking on, can provide a solid foundation for navigating uncertainty. By letting go of our need for control and surrendering to the ouch of life, we allow ourselves to adapt and respond to changes with grace.

Resilience is another essential quality in embracing uncertainty. It is the ability to bounce back from setbacks and challenges, and to continue moving forward despite the unknown. By cultivating resilience, we can face uncertainty head-on, learning from our failures and using them as stepping stones towards success. This part of the work also provides practical strategies and insights on how to build resilience in the face of uncertainty.

Furthermore, embracing uncertainty with grace and resilience requires us to cultivate a sense of mindfulness and presence. By being fully present in the moment, we can let go of worries about the future and regrets about the past. This allows us to focus on what truly matters, making conscious choices and decisions that align with our values and goals.

Through personal anecdotes, expert interviews, and practical exercises, this subchapter will guide parents and business owners on a transformative journey towards embracing uncertainty with grace and resilience. By incorporating spiritual sanity into our lives, we can find inner peace, balance, and fulfillment amidst the chaos of uncertainty. Together, let us embark on the path to harmony, embracing uncertainty as an opportunity for growth and transformation.

6.3 Courage to Accept Change

In our journey through life, change is the only constant. As parents and business owners, we are often faced with numerous challenges and unexpected turns that can leave us feeling overwhelmed and uncertain. It is during these times that we must find the courage to accept change and embrace it as an opportunity for growth and transformation. Change can be scary, especially when it disrupts the balance and stability, we have worked so hard to achieve. However, it is important to remember that change is not inherently negative or destructive. Rather, it is a natural part of our evolution as individuals and as businesses. By embracing change, we open ourselves up to new possibilities and experiences that can enrich our lives and propel us towards success.

To find the courage to accept change, we must first cultivate a mindset of resilience and adaptability. This means letting go of rigid expectations and embracing the unknown with an open mind and heart. It requires us to trust in our own abilities and to believe that we have the strength to navigate through whatever challenges come our way.

In the realm of parenting, change can manifest in various ways. From the physical and emotional growth of our children to the shifting dynamics within our family structure, change is inevitable. By accepting and embracing these changes, we can create a nurturing and supportive environment that fosters the healthy development of our children.

Similarly, in the world of business, change is a constant force that demands our attention and adaptability. Whether it is a shift in market trends, technological advancements, or the need for innovation, the ability to accept and embrace change is crucial for sustainable growth and success.

Finding spiritual sanity amidst the chaos of change is a journey that requires self-reflection, mindfulness, and a deep connection to our inner selves. By cultivating a spiritual practice, whether through meditation, prayer, or other forms of self-care, we can find the clarity and strength to navigate through the challenges that change brings.

The courage to accept change is not a one-time act, but rather a continuous practice. It requires us to let go of fear, embrace uncertainty, and trust in the process of life. By doing so, we open ourselves up to new opportunities, growth, and ultimately, a path to harmony in both our personal and professional lives.

In conclusion, as parents and business owners, the courage to accept change is essential for our own sanity and well-being. By embracing change as an opportunity for growth, we can create a harmonious balance between our spiritual selves and the challenges that life presents. Let us find the courage within ourselves to accept change and embrace the journey towards spiritual sanity.

CHAPTER 7: FINDING SUPPORT AND COMMUNITY

Navigating the intricate terrain of parenthood and business ownership, Chapter 6 illuminates the art of 'Adapting to Transitions.' As William Bridges, a foremost expert on managing change, posits, transitions are not merely about external shifts but internal transformations. The chapter intricately weaves insights from Bridges' work into the fabric of parenting and entrepreneurship, guiding individuals through the intricate dance of embracing change. Drawing parallels between Bridges' emphasis on self-care during transitions and the demands of parenting and business, the chapter unveils a holistic approach. Inspired by the transformative potential in transitions, the chapter echoes the sentiment of Bridges, urging individuals to prioritize their well-being, foster flexibility, and seek support to maintain spiritual sanity during moments of change.

In the face of the inescapable uncertainties that punctuate contemporary life, Chapter 6 unravels the profound narrative of 'Embracing Uncertainty with Grace and Resilience.' Rooted in the teachings of mindfulness luminaries like Jon Kabat-Zinn, the chapter champions the idea that uncertainty, rather than a source of fear, can be an avenue for growth and self-discovery. By infusing the wisdom of Kabat-Zinn into the challenges faced by parents and business owners, the chapter guides individuals towards cultivating trust, resilience, and mindfulness. It strategically incorporates practical strategies, echoing Kabat-Zinn's stress reduction methods, to empower individuals in the art of navigating uncertainty with poise and resilience. The chapter serves as a transformative guide, encouraging parents and business owners to view uncertainty not as an obstacle but as a catalyst for spiritual growth and transformation.

Finally, in the perpetual ebb and flow of life, change stands as an unwavering constant. This Chapter resonates with the wisdom of those who recognize change as an opportunity for growth and transformation. Intertwining the insights of thought leaders like Viktor Frankl and the practical philosophy of resilience, the chapter champions the courage to embrace change. In both parenting and business, the chapter draws on the wisdom of acknowledging change not as a disruption but as a catalyst for evolution. Inspired by Frankl's logotherapy, the chapter delves into the realms of finding spiritual sanity amidst change, emphasizing the importance of self-reflection and mindfulness practices. As parents and business owners stand at the crossroads of uncertainty, this chapter empowers them to find the courage to accept change as an integral part of their journey toward harmonious well-being.

7.1 Seeking Supportive Networks and Resources

It is crucial for parents and business owners to maintain a sense of spiritual sanity because balancing the responsibilities of parenthood and running a business can be overwhelming, and it is easy to feel isolated and disconnected from our spiritual selves. However, there is a solution: seeking supportive networks and resources that can help us navigate this journey with grace and harmony. Some Steps are crucial here.

1. *Recognizing the Importance of Community*: This is one of the first steps towards finding spiritual sanity. As parents and business owners, we often feel the weight of the world on our shoulders. However, by reaching out and connecting with like-minded individuals, we can find solace and support. This can include joining local parenting groups, attending business networking events, or even participating in online forums and communities. By surrounding ourselves with individuals who understand our unique challenges, we can find comfort in knowing that we are not alone.

2. *Seeking out Inspirational Resources*: It is essential to seek out resources that can inspire and guide us on our spiritual journey.

Books, podcasts, and workshops can provide valuable insights and practical tools for navigating the complexities of parenthood and business ownership. These resources can help us tap into our inner wisdom and find a sense of peace amidst the chaos. Whether it is a book on mindfulness practices or a podcast on conscious parenting, these resources can serve as a guiding light on our path to spiritual sanity.

3. *Seeking professional support*: This can be immensely beneficial. Engaging the services of a life coach or therapist who specializes in working with parents and business owners can provide us with the necessary tools and techniques to manage stress, set boundaries, and maintain a healthy work-life balance. These professionals can offer a safe space for us to explore our fears, challenges, and aspirations, guiding us towards a state of spiritual sanity.

4. *Find Supportive Networks*: It is important to remember that seeking supportive networks and resources is not a sign of weakness, but rather a testament to our commitment to personal growth and well-being. By surrounding ourselves with a community of like-minded individuals and accessing valuable resources, we can find the strength and resilience to navigate the challenges of parenthood and business ownership while staying connected to our spiritual selves.

In conclusion, seeking supportive networks and resources is essential for parents and business owners who aspire to maintain spiritual sanity. By connecting with others, accessing valuable resources, and seeking professional support, we can find solace, guidance, and inspiration on our journey towards harmony. Let us embrace the power of community and knowledge, as we navigate the intricate dance of parenthood, business ownership, and spiritual well-being.

7.2 Creating a Supportive Environment for Growth and Harmony

Very often, parents and business owners find themselves navigating through the chaos and stress of daily life. The constant juggling act of managing responsibilities at home and at work can leave us feeling overwhelmed and disconnected from our true selves. In the pursuit of success, we sometimes neglect our well-being and the well-being of those around us. However, it is crucial to understand that growth and harmony can only thrive in a supportive environment.

In our journey towards spiritual sanity, we must recognize the importance of creating a nurturing space that fosters growth and harmony. This subchapter aims to guide parents and business owners in cultivating an environment that allows for personal and professional development while maintaining a sense of balance and peace.

Firstly, it is essential to prioritize self-care. As parents and business owners, we often put the needs of others before our own. However, neglecting our own well-being will ultimately hinder our ability to provide support and guidance to those who depend on us. By practicing self-care, whether it be through meditation, exercise, or engaging in hobbies we enjoy, we replenish our energy and create a positive example for our children and colleagues.

Secondly, fostering open and honest communication is crucial in maintaining harmony within our personal and professional relationships. Encouraging dialogue and creating a safe space for others to express their thoughts and feelings fosters trust and understanding. By actively listening and respecting diverse perspectives, we create an environment that values growth and collaboration.

Thirdly, it is important to set clear boundaries and expectations. As parents, we must establish consistent discipline methods that promote growth and learning in our children. In the business world, setting clear expectations and boundaries with our employees and partners creates a sense of structure and accountability. By doing so, we create an environment that encourages personal and professional development while maintaining a harmonious atmosphere.

Fourthly, embracing gratitude and mindfulness is essential in creating a supportive environment. By practicing gratitude, we cultivate a positive mindset and acknowledge the blessings in our lives. Mindfulness allows us to be fully present in our interactions and appreciate the beauty around us. By incorporating these practices into our daily lives, we create a supportive environment that fosters growth, harmony, and spiritual sanity.

In conclusion, creating a supportive environment for growth and harmony is essential for parents and business owners seeking spiritual sanity. By prioritizing self-care, fostering open communication, setting clear boundaries, and embracing gratitude and mindfulness, we create a nurturing space that allows for personal and professional development. In this environment, both ourselves and those around us can thrive and find true harmony in our lives.

7.3 The Role of Family and Friends

In our journey towards achieving spiritual sanity as parents and business owners, the role of family and friends cannot be underestimated. They are the pillars of support, the guiding light, and the source of strength in our lives. Our loved ones play a crucial role in helping us maintain a harmonious balance between our personal and professional lives, enabling us to find peace and fulfillment in our spiritual journey.

Family is the foundation upon which our lives are built. They provide us with unconditional love, support, and encouragement. As parents, our families are our first teachers, helping us shape our values, beliefs, and attitudes. They offer a safe haven where we can freely express ourselves and seek solace during challenging times. It is through our families that we learn the importance of empathy, compassion, and forgiveness, which are essential elements of maintaining spiritual sanity.

Our friends, too, play an integral role in our pursuit of spiritual sanity. They are the ones who understand us, accept us, and provide a non-judgmental space for us to grow. True friends are like-minded individuals who share our spiritual journey and provide us with the necessary support and guidance. They inspire us, challenge us, and remind us of our purpose when we lose sight of it. Through their wisdom and experiences, they help us navigate the complexities of life and align our spiritual goals with our personal and professional aspirations.

As parents and business owners, it is vital to cultivate strong relationships with our families and friends. We must create a harmonious environment where our loved ones feel valued, heard, and respected. Regular communication, quality time spent together, and nurturing shared interests and traditions are all ways to strengthen these bonds. By prioritizing our relationships, we not only enhance our own spiritual well-being but also set an example for our children and colleagues on the importance of fostering meaningful connections.

Finally, the role of family and friends in our pursuit of spiritual sanity cannot be emphasized enough. They are the anchors that keep us grounded, the sources of love and support that enable us to maintain balance, and the guiding lights that illuminate our path. By investing in our relationships and cherishing the bonds we share, we create a nurturing environment that fosters our spiritual growth as parents and business owners. Let us treasure our families and friends, for they are the true blessings on our journey towards harmony and spiritual sanity.

CHAPTER 8: SPIRITUAL PRACTICES FOR PARENTS AND BUSINESS OWNERS

Embarking on a transformative exploration, this chapter unravels the profound impact of incorporating 'Spiritual Practices for Parents and Business Owners.' Delving into the expert-guided realm of mindfulness and spiritual grounding, it draws insights from renowned figures like Jon Kabat-Zinn, the chapter elucidates how meditation becomes a poignant practice, offering parents and business owners a respite from the relentless demands of life. By dedicating mere minutes to meditation, individuals tap into their intuition, gaining clarity and wisdom. In addition, the chapter emphasizes the potency of prayer, echoing the spiritual insights of various belief systems, underscoring its role in providing strength, comfort, and clarity for both parents and business owners by highlighting the transformative potential of giving back.

Inspired by the teachings of compassion and empathy, it illuminates how parents can instil these values in their children through early engagement in charitable acts. For business owners, charity and volunteer services become avenues to create positive workplace cultures and enhance brand images, reinforcing the significance of giving, not only for personal fulfillment but also as a means to contribute to a harmonious society. Through these practices, the chapter constructs a roadmap, urging individuals to integrate moments of stillness and heartfelt connection into their daily lives, fostering a profound sense of inner peace and harmony.

8.1 Meditation and Prayer for Connection and Clarity

Balancing the demands of family life and professional responsibilities can be challenging, leaving little time for self-reflection and personal growth. However, incorporating meditation and prayer into daily routines can be a powerful tool for finding spiritual sanity amidst the chaos.

Meditation is the practice of quieting the mind and focusing on the present moment. It allows us to cultivate a sense of inner peace and stillness, even in the midst of a hectic schedule. By setting aside just a few minutes each day for meditation, parents and business owners can find a sense of clarity and connection to their true selves.

Through meditation, we can tap into our intuition and gain valuable insights into our lives. It provides a space for reflection, allowing us to step back from the constant noise and busyness and access a deeper understanding of ourselves and the world around us. This newfound clarity can help parents make better decisions for their families and business owners navigate challenges with greater wisdom and discernment.

In addition to meditation, prayer is another powerful tool for spiritual sanity. Prayer is a way to connect with a higher power, whether it be God, the universe, or any other spiritual belief system. It allows us to express our gratitude, seek guidance, and find solace in times of difficulty.

For parents, prayer can be a way to find strength and guidance in raising children. It can provide a sense of comfort and reassurance, knowing that there is a higher power looking out for their family. Similarly, business owners can turn to prayer to seek clarity and inspiration in their professional endeavours. By surrendering their worries and concerns to a higher power, they can find peace and trust in the process.

By incorporating meditation and prayer into their daily lives, parents and business owners can cultivate a sense of spiritual sanity. These practices provide a much-needed respite from the constant demands of life, allowing individuals to reconnect with their true selves and find clarity amidst the chaos. Whether it is through moments of stillness in meditation or heartfelt conversations in prayer, these practices offer a path to inner peace and harmony in both personal and professional spheres.

In the end, the subchapter 'Meditation and Prayer for Connection and Clarity' offers parents and business owners a roadmap to finding spiritual sanity. By dedicating time to quiet the mind through meditation and connecting with a higher power through prayer, individuals can gain clarity, make better decisions, and find a sense of peace amidst the chaos of daily life. These practices provide a foundation for personal growth, allowing individuals to navigate the challenges of parenthood and business ownership with greater wisdom and grace.

8.2 Incorporating Rituals and Traditions in Daily Life

Rituals and traditions have a profound impact on our lives. They provide a sense of stability, connection, and meaning in an increasingly fast-paced and chaotic world. Whether you are a parent juggling the demands of family life or a business owner striving for success, incorporating rituals and traditions into your daily routine can be a powerful tool for achieving spiritual sanity.

For parents, creating rituals and traditions within the family can foster a sense of belonging and unity. They help to create a safe and secure environment where children can thrive. Simple acts like sharing a meal together every evening, reading bedtime stories, or engaging in a weekly family outing can become cherished rituals that strengthen the bonds within the family. These rituals not only provide a sense of structure but also offer opportunities for open communication and quality time spent together.

Similarly, business owners can benefit from incorporating rituals and traditions into their daily lives. In the fast-paced and competitive business world, it is easy to become overwhelmed and lose sight of the bigger picture. By establishing daily or weekly rituals, such as mindful meditation or a morning gratitude practice, business owners can ground themselves and maintain a sense of balance. These rituals help to reduce stress, increase focus, and foster creativity, ultimately leading to improved decision-making and overall success.

Incorporating rituals and traditions into daily life is not limited to specific activities but also extends to special occasions and celebrations. Creating traditions around holidays, birthdays, or milestones can bring joy and excitement to both family and business settings. These traditions can be as simple as decorating the office for a special occasion or hosting an annual family gathering. Such celebrations provide an opportunity to pause, reflect, and express gratitude for the journey travelled thus far.

In a world that often prioritizes productivity and material success, incorporating rituals and traditions into daily life allows parents and business owners to reconnect with their spiritual selves. These practices remind us of the importance of being present, nurturing relationships, and finding meaning beyond the daily grind. By embracing rituals and traditions, individuals can achieve spiritual sanity, leading to a more fulfilling and harmonious life for themselves and those around them.

Finally, whether you are a parent or a business owner, incorporating rituals and traditions into your daily life is essential for achieving spiritual sanity. These practices provide a sense of stability, connection, and meaning that can nurture both personal and professional growth. By creating rituals within the family or workplace and celebrating special occasions, individuals can find balance, reduce stress, and foster a sense of unity. Embracing rituals and traditions allows us to reconnect with our spiritual selves and cultivate a more fulfilling and harmonious life.

8.3 Charity and Volunteer Services

In today's fast-paced and materialistic world, it is easy for parents and business owners to get caught up in the pursuit of success and forget about the importance of giving back. However, embracing charity and volunteer services can be a powerful tool for achieving spiritual sanity amidst the chaos of daily life.

For parents, teaching their children the value of charity and volunteerism is of utmost importance. By involving their kids in acts of giving and volunteering from an early age, parents can instill in them a sense of compassion, empathy, and gratitude. Engaging in charity work as a family not only strengthens the bond between parents and children but also provides an opportunity for spiritual growth and understanding.

Business owners, on the other hand, have a unique platform to make a significant impact through their philanthropic efforts. Incorporating charity and volunteer services into their business model can not only enhance their brand image but also create a positive workplace culture. By encouraging employees to participate in volunteering activities, business owners can foster a sense of unity and purpose within their organizations. Moreover, engaging in charitable initiatives can serve as a source of inspiration and motivation, injecting a sense of fulfillment and meaning into their professional lives.

Engaging in charity and volunteer services is not only beneficial for parents and business owners personally but also for the community at large. By extending a helping hand to those in need, individuals can contribute to the creation of a harmonious society. Whether it is through donating money, time, or skills, every act of charity plays a role in alleviating suffering and bringing joy to others. Moreover, the act of giving can bring a sense of fulfillment and purpose, ultimately leading to a state of spiritual sanity.

To fully embrace the power of charity and volunteer services, parents and business owners must prioritize these activities in their lives. By setting aside dedicated time for volunteering, individuals can make a conscious effort to give back regularly. It is crucial to remember that charity does not always have to involve grand gestures or significant financial contributions. Simple acts of kindness, such as helping a neighbor or offering support to a colleague, can also have a profound impact on others and contribute to personal growth and spiritual well-being.

It is good to note in conclusion that, charity and volunteer services are essential components of achieving spiritual sanity for parents and business owners. By embracing these practices, individuals can cultivate compassion, empathy, and gratitude in themselves and their children. Moreover, incorporating philanthropy into business models can create a positive workplace culture and enhance brand image. Ultimately, acts of giving contribute to the betterment of society and bring a sense of fulfillment and purpose to those who engage in them.

CHAPTER 9: INTEGRATING SPIRITUALITY INTO PARENTING AND BUSINESS

This chapter zooms in on 'Integrating Spirituality into Parenting and Business,' which serves as guides to parents and business owners toward a harmonious balance. It also navigates the intricate terrain of ethical decision-making, referencing experts like Mary Gentile, known for her work on value-driven leadership. It underscores the importance of aligning personal and business values, infusing ethical principles into decision-making processes, and fostering a sense of spiritual sanity. The chapter further draws on the wisdom of various experts to explore the interplay between personal values, ethical business practices, and the cultivation of a purposeful business model.

The subchapter focuses on 'Creating a Purposeful and Ethical Business Model, advocating for a holistic approach to success and spiritual sanity, citing business experts like Simon Sinek. It further delves into the intricacies of aligning personal values with business objectives, upholding ethical standards, and embracing social and environmental responsibility. The narrative emphasizes the continuous self-reflection required for creating a business model that not only thrives financially but also contributes to a greater purpose.

Furthermore, it throws light on 'Practical Reflection of Spirituality,' acknowledging the challenges parents and business owners face in maintaining sanity amidst daily chaos. Referencing the importance of mindfulness, gratitude, and community, the chapter provides practical insights inspired by renowned figures like Jon Kabat-Zinn and Brene Brown. The chapter unfolds a roadmap for individuals to practically incorporate spirituality into their lives, promoting self-care, setting boundaries, and fostering connections.

9.1 Fostering Values and Ethics in Parenting and Business Decisions

As parents and business owners, we often find ourselves faced with difficult decisions that can have a significant impact on our families and the well-being of our businesses. So, how can we navigate this delicate path and ensure we are fostering values and ethics in both our parenting and business decisions?

In *The Path to Harmony: Spiritual Sanity for Parents and Business Owners*, we delve into the importance of nurturing our spiritual sanity to guide us in making ethical choices that resonate with our values. This subchapter explores the vital role that values and ethics play in our roles as parents and business owners, offering practical insights and strategies to cultivate a harmonious balance.

As parents, our primary responsibility is to instil values and ethics in our children. By setting a positive example and fostering open and honest communication, we can teach them the importance of integrity, empathy, and compassion. We discuss how to create a home environment that encourages these values, emphasizing the significance of active listening and modelling ethical behaviour.

Simultaneously, as business owners, we have a duty to make decisions that align with our core values and ethical principles. This part of the work explores the challenges of ethical decision making in the corporate world and provides guidance on maintaining integrity while pursuing success. We discuss the importance of transparency, fairness, and social responsibility, showing how these values can positively impact our businesses and the wider community.

Furthermore, we delve into the concept of spiritual sanity, emphasizing the significance of nurturing our inner selves to make sound ethical decisions. We explore practices such as mindfulness, meditation, and reflection, which can help us connect with our values and make conscious choices aligned with our spiritual beliefs.

The Path to Harmony: Spiritual Sanity for Parents and Business Owners offers a holistic approach to fostering values and ethics in both parenting and business decisions. By integrating our spiritual selves into our roles as parents and business owners, we can cultivate a harmonious balance that prioritizes the well-being of our families, ourselves, and our businesses. Join us on this transformative journey towards spiritual sanity and discover the rewards of living a life guided by integrity, compassion, and ethical decision-making.

9.2 Creating a Purposeful and Ethical Business Model

In a competitive world like ours today, it is crucial for parents and business owners to not only achieve success but also maintain a sense of spiritual sanity. The concept of spirituality in business may seem unconventional, but incorporating ethical practices and a purposeful business model can bring about a harmonious balance between personal values and professional success. This subchapter will delve into the importance of creating a purposeful and ethical business model, providing valuable insights and practical tips for parents and business owners seeking spiritual sanity in their endeavors.

1. *Aligning Personal Values and Objectives*: At the core of a purposeful business model lies the alignment of personal values and business objectives. Parents and business owners must introspect and identify their core values, beliefs, and passions. Understanding these aspects will serve as a compass, guiding decisions and actions towards a more meaningful and purpose driven business. By infusing personal values into the business model, individuals can create a sense of fulfillment and authenticity, which will resonate with customers and employees alike.

2. *Adherence to Ethical Standards*: Ethics form the foundation of a purposeful business model. It is essential to establish a set of ethical guidelines that govern all business operations. This includes fair treatment of employees, transparency in financial dealings, and responsible sourcing and production. By adhering to ethical standards, parents and business owners not only foster a positive work environment but also earn the trust and loyalty of customers.

3. *Social and Environmental Responsibility*: In addition to ethics, social and environmental responsibility should also be integrated into the business model. Sustainable practices, such as reducing waste, utilizing renewable resources, and supporting local communities, not only benefit the planet but also enhance the reputation of the business. Parents and business owners can play a vital role in creating a better world by incorporating these practices into their daily operations.

Creating a purposeful and ethical business model requires continuous self-reflection and improvement. It involves actively seeking feedback from customers, employees, and stakeholders to identify areas for growth and refinement. By listening and adapting to the needs and expectations of others, parents and business owners can foster a culture of collaboration and inclusivity.

Conclusively, creating a purposeful and ethical business model is instrumental in achieving spiritual sanity for parents and business owners. By aligning personal values with business objectives, adhering to ethical guidelines, and embracing social and environmental responsibility, individuals can create a harmonious balance between their personal and professional lives. This subchapter provides practical insights and guidance for those seeking to create a business that not only brings financial success but also contributes to a greater purpose.

9.3 Practical Reflection of Spirituality

Even though it can be challenging for parents and business owners to find a sense of sanity amidst the chaos of daily engagements, it is possible. It is in fact precisely during these times that the need for spirituality becomes even more crucial. This subchapter "Practical Reflection of Spirituality" in this book, *The Path to Harmony: Spiritual Sanity for Parents and Business Owners*, aims to provide valuable insights and guidance to help parents and business owners nurture their spiritual well-being and find balance in their lives.

Although spirituality is often associated with religious practices, yet it goes beyond that, it is not limited to it alone. It involves connecting with something greater than ourselves, finding meaning and purpose, and cultivating inner peace. In this subchapter, we explore how individuals can practically incorporate spirituality into their hectic lives.

One practical reflection of spirituality is the practice of mindfulness earlier accentuated. This is important because it involves being fully present in the moment, paying attention to our thoughts, emotions, and physical sensations without judgment. By incorporating mindfulness into our daily routines, we can become more aware of our actions, make conscious choices, and reduce stress.

Another practical aspect of spirituality is the cultivation of gratitude. Gratitude is a powerful tool that can shift our focus from what is lacking to what is already abundant in our lives. By regularly reflecting on the things we are grateful for, we can develop a positive mindset and increase our overall well-being.

Moreover, we delve into the importance of self-care and setting boundaries. As parents and business owners, it is easy to get caught up in responsibilities and neglect our own needs. However, by prioritizing self-care activities such as exercise, meditation, and hobbies, we can recharge our energy and enhance our spiritual well-being. Setting boundaries is equally essential to prevent burnout and maintain a healthy work-life balance.

Furthermore, we explore the importance of community and connection in spirituality. Being part of a supportive and like-minded community can provide a sense of belonging and understanding. We discuss practical ways to foster these connections, such as joining local spiritual groups, attending workshops, or participating in online forums.

Finally, the subchapter offers parents and business owners practical and achievable strategies to incorporate spirituality into their lives. By embracing mindfulness, gratitude, self-care, setting boundaries, and fostering connections, individuals can find spiritual sanity, balance, and inner peace in the midst of their hectic lives. Our book aims to guide readers on their path to harmony, empowering them to navigate the challenges of parenting and business ownership with a grounded and spiritual mindset.

CHAPTER 10: SUSTAINING SPIRITUAL SANITY

In the intricate dance of parenting and business ownership, maintaining spiritual sanity is a delicate yet imperative task. This last Chapter explores effective strategies to navigate the challenges faced by the dynamic landscape of contemporary life, where the responsibilities of parenting and entrepreneurship often intersect, bearing in mind that achieving balance and harmony becomes paramount for maintaining spiritual sanity. Drawing on the expertise of mindfulness advocates like Jon Kabat-Zinn and organizational experts like Simon Sinek, the subchapter 'Strategies for Maintaining Balance and Harmony' unfolds a roadmap to prioritize self-care, set clear boundaries, practice mindfulness, cultivate support systems, schedule quality time, and embrace imperfection. Rooted in practicality, these strategies offer a solid foundation for spiritual sanity, enabling individuals to gracefully manage the intricacies of parenthood and entrepreneurship. It further throws light on the 'Long-Term Growth and Sustainability in Parenting and Business,' the narrative delves into the achievable prospect of sustained growth and spiritual fulfillment in both realms. Referencing insights from renowned figures like Brene Brown, the chapter advocates for aligning personal values with business objectives, adopting ethical practices, and fostering self-reflection to create a legacy extending beyond immediate spheres of influence.

Finally, it deepens with 'Continuous Practice,' emphasizing the transformative power of intentional spiritual habits. Inspired by mindfulness experts like Jon Kabat-Zinn, the subchapter underscores the significance of present-moment awareness, self-reflection, and meaningful rituals. It positions continuous practice as a guiding light, enabling parents and business owners to restore harmony, find solace, and foster spiritual well-being amidst the constant demands of their roles. The focus on 'Sustaining Spiritual Sanity,' further invites readers on a journey of continuous growth, resilience, and self-discovery. By embracing practical strategies and cultivating intentional spiritual practices, individuals can not only navigate the complexities of their roles but also foster a legacy of harmonious living and spiritual fulfillment.

10.1 Strategies for Maintaining Balance and Harmony

Given the nature of today's fast-changing world where the demands of parenting and running a business can often collide, finding balance and harmony becomes essential for maintaining spiritual sanity. This subchapter explores effective strategies that can help parents and business owners navigate the challenges and achieve a sense of equilibrium in their lives.

1. *Prioritize Self-Care*: It is crucial to remember that taking care of oneself is not selfish, but rather a necessary foundation for maintaining balance. Parents and business owners should prioritize self-care activities such as exercise, meditation, or hobbies that bring them joy and rejuvenate their spirits. By nurturing themselves, they can better care for others and handle the demands of their responsibilities.

2. *Setting Clear Boundaries*: Establishing boundaries is essential for maintaining balance and harmony. Parents and business owners should define their limits in terms of work hours, family time, and personal space. Learning to say no when necessary and delegating tasks can help prevent burnout and ensure that both family and business receive the attention they deserve.

3. *Practicing Mindfulness*: Incorporating mindfulness into daily life can be transformative. By being fully present in the moment, parents and business owners can enhance their focus, reduce stress, and improve decision-making. Mindfulness exercises such as deep breathing, visualization, or simple awareness of the present moment can help restore balance and promote a sense of inner peace.

4. *Cultivating Support Systems*: Building a strong support network is vital for maintaining balance. Parents and business owners should surround themselves with individuals who understand their unique challenges and offer guidance and encouragement. This can include joining support groups, seeking mentorship, or engaging in networking activities that foster connections with like-minded individuals.

5. *Scheduling Quality Time*: Carving out dedicated quality time for family, loved ones, and oneself is essential for maintaining harmony. Parents and business owners should schedule regular family activities, date nights, and personal retreats to recharge and strengthen relationships. This intentional focus on quality time fosters deeper connections, cultivates emotional well-being, and enhances overall life satisfaction.

6. *Embracing Imperfection*: Accepting that perfection is unattainable is a key step in achieving balance and harmony. Parents and business owners should let go of unrealistic expectations and embrace imperfections. Recognizing that mistakes happen and that learning from them is part of the journey can alleviate unnecessary stress and help foster a more balanced perspective.

By implementing these strategies, parents and business owners can create a solid foundation for maintaining balance and harmony in their lives. These practices can lead to a greater sense of spiritual sanity, enabling individuals to navigate the challenges of parenthood and entrepreneurship with grace and mindfulness. Remember, it is through achieving harmony within ourselves that we can best serve our families and businesses.

10. 2 Long-term Growth and Sustainability in Parenting and Business

Despite the difficulty in achieving a balance owing to the demands of the roles of a parent and a business owner combined in one person, it is to be noted that it is not impossible. Daunting as the task may appear to be, achieving long-term growth and sustainability in both parenting and business is not only possible but can also bring about a sense of spiritual sanity.

As parents, it is crucial to recognize that our children are not only a precious gift but also our future. Nurturing their growth and development requires a deep understanding of their needs and aspirations. This involves creating a harmonious environment where love, respect, and guidance coexist. By fostering open communication and setting clear boundaries, we can establish a strong foundation for our children's emotional and spiritual well-being.

Similarly, in the realm of business, achieving sustainable growth requires a holistic approach. It is essential to align our values and beliefs with our business practices. By adopting ethical and sustainable business strategies, we can create a positive impact on society and the environment. This not only benefits our stakeholders but also brings a sense of fulfillment and spiritual satisfaction.

Finding harmony between parenting and business is a continuous process that requires self-reflection and adaptation. It is important to prioritize self-care and maintain a healthy work-life balance. Taking time for introspection, meditation, and connecting with our inner selves can provide clarity and guidance in both our parenting and business decisions.

In this subchapter, 'Long-term Growth and Sustainability in Parenting and Business,' we explore various strategies and practices that can help parents and business owners achieve spiritual sanity. We delve into the importance of setting realistic goals, developing effective time management techniques, and fostering a supportive network of like-minded individuals.

Moreover, we discuss the significance of embracing change and cultivating resilience in the face of challenges. By staying adaptable and open to new opportunities, we can find innovative solutions that benefit both our families and businesses.

Ultimately, the path to harmony lies in acknowledging the interconnectedness of our roles as parents and business owners. By embracing spiritual sanity, we can cultivate long-term growth and sustainability in both aspects of our lives, creating a legacy that extends far beyond our immediate spheres of influence.

10.3 Continuous Practice

In the pursuit of spiritual sanity, parents and business owners often find themselves overwhelmed by the demands of their roles. The constant switching act between family responsibilities and professional commitments can leave little room for personal growth and inner peace. However, amidst the chaos of daily life, there lies a powerful tool that can help restore harmony and balance – continuous practice.

Continuous practice refers to the intentional cultivation of spiritual habits and routines that nurture our inner selves. It is through consistent and dedicated practice that we can find solace, clarity, and resilience in the face of challenges. Whether you are a parent striving to create a nurturing environment for your children or a business owner seeking to lead with compassion and integrity, continuous practice can be your guiding light on the path to harmonious living.

One of the cornerstones of continuous practice is mindfulness. By cultivating present-moment awareness, we can learn to fully engage with our surroundings, relationships, and tasks at hand. Mindfulness allows us to let go of distractions and connect with the essence of each moment. Through practices such as meditation, breathwork, and body awareness exercises, we can train our minds to be fully present, enabling us to make conscious choices and respond to situations with clarity and calmness.

Another important aspect of continuous practice is self-reflection. Taking time to reflect on our thoughts, emotions, and actions provides valuable insights into our inner world. By journaling, engaging in introspective exercises, or seeking guidance from mentors or therapists, we can gain a deeper understanding of ourselves and our patterns. This self-awareness empowers us to make conscious changes, aligning our actions with our values and intentions.

Additionally, continuous practice involves incorporating rituals and routines that nourish our spirits. These can range from simple acts such as lighting a candle, practicing gratitude, or reading inspirational texts, to more elaborate rituals like creating sacred spaces or participating in group ceremonies. Engaging in these practices regularly helps us reconnect with our inner wisdom, fostering a sense of purpose and fulfillment.

It is important to remember that continuous practice is not about perfection but rather about progress. It is an ongoing journey of self-discovery and growth, with its own ebb and ouch. By embracing this mindset, parents and business owners can navigate the challenges of their respective roles with grace and resilience. Through continuous practice, we can cultivate spiritual sanity, finding harmony within ourselves and inspiring those around us.

CONCLUSION

It is all too easy for parents and business owners to become overwhelmed and lose sight of their own well-being in the business of the world today. The pursuit of success, whether in our careers or in raising our children, can often lead to a neglect of our spiritual selves. However, it is essential for our overall happiness and fulfillment that we embrace the journey of spiritual sanity.

Throughout this book, *The Path to Harmony: Spiritual Sanity for Parents and Business Owners*, we have explored the importance of finding balance and aligning our spiritual and worldly responsibilities. We have delved into various practices and techniques that can help us navigate the challenges of modern life with grace and peace. As parents, it is crucial that we recognize the impact our own spiritual well-being has on our children. By nurturing our own souls, we create a harmonious environment that allows our children to thrive. We have learned that finding time for self-reflection, meditation, and self-care is not selfish but rather a necessary investment in our family's overall happiness.

Similarly, as business owners, embracing spiritual sanity enables us to lead with compassion, integrity, and purpose. By aligning our values with our professional endeavors, we can create a positive impact on our employees, customers, and the world at large. We have discovered that when we prioritize our spiritual well-being, not only do we enhance our own success, but we also inspire and uplift those around us. The journey of spiritual sanity is not a destination but an ongoing process. It requires dedication, self-awareness, and a willingness to let go of control. As parents and business owners, we must be open to embracing new perspectives, exploring different spiritual practices, and seeking support from like-minded individuals or mentors.

Finally, the path to spiritual sanity is a transformative journey that allows us to find harmony between our personal and professional lives. By prioritizing our spiritual well-being, we can create a nurturing environment for our families, foster success in our businesses, and ultimately find fulfillment and peace within ourselves. With the right discipline, we can achieve this. So, let us embark on this journey together, as parents and business owners, and embrace the path to spiritual sanity. May it lead us to a life of balance, joy, and purpose, and may we inspire others to do the same.

REFERENCES

Branson, R. (2011). *Screw Business as Usual*. Penguin.

Bridges, W. (2004). *Transitions: Making Sense of Life's Changes*. Da Capo Press.

Bridges, W. (2009). *Managing Transitions: Making the Most of Change*. Da Capo Lifelong Books.

Brown, B. (2010). *The Gifts of Imperfection: Let Go of Who You Think You're Supposed to Be and Embrace Who You Are*. Hazelden Publishing.

Brown, S. (2009). *Play: How it Shapes the Brain, Opens the Imagination, and Invigorates the Soul*. Penguin.

Chödrön, P. (2002). *When Things Fall Apart: Heart Advice for Difficult Times*. Shambhala Publications.

Cloud, H. (1992). *Boundaries: When to Say Yes, How to Say No to Take Control of Your Life*. Zondervan.

Courage to Accept Change

Covey, S. R. (1989). *The 7 Habits of Highly Effective People*. Simon & Schuster.

Dyer, W. (1976). *Your Erroneous Zones*. HarperCollins.

Frankl, V. E. (1946). Man's Search for Meaning. Beacon Press.

Gardner, H. (1985). *Frames of Mind: The Theory of Multiple Intelligences*. Basic Books.

Gottman, J., & Silver, N. (1999). *The Seven Principles for Making Marriage Work*. Harmony.

Hanson, R., & Mendius, R. (2009). *The Practical Neuroscience of Buddha's Brain: Happiness, Love & Wisdom*. New Harbinger Publications.

Huffington, A. (2016). *The Sleep Revolution: Transforming Your Life, One Night at a Time*. Harmony. Hanh, T. N. (2012). *The Art of Communicating*. HarperOne.

Johnson, S. M. (2008). *Hold Me Tight: Seven Conversations for a Lifetime of Love*. Little, Brown and Company.

Kabat-Zinn, J. (1990). *Full Catastrophe Living: Using the Wisdom of Your Body and Mind to Face Stress*, Pain, and Illness. Bantam.

Kabat-Zinn, J. (1994). *Wherever You Go, There You Are: Mindfulness Meditation in Everyday Life*. Hachette Books.

Kabat-Zinn, J. (1994). *Wherever You Go, There You Are: Mindfulness Meditation in Everyday Life*. Hachette Books.

Kotter, J. P. (1996). *Leading Change*. Harvard Business Review Press.

Langer, E. (1989). *Mindfulness*. Da Capo Lifelong Books.

Misner, I. (1985). *The World's Best-Known Marketing Secret: Building Your Business with Word-of-Mouth Marketing*. Bard Press.

Rosenberg, M. B. (2003). *Nonviolent Communication: A Language of Life*. PuddleDancer Press.

Siegel, D. (2012). *The Whole-Brain Child: 12 Revolutionary Strategies to Nurture Your Child's Developing Mind*. Bantam.

Tsabary, S. (2013). *The Conscious Parent: Transforming Ourselves, Empowering Our Children*. Namaste Publishing.

Walker, M. (2017). *Why We Sleep*: Unlocking the Power of Sleep and Dreams. Scribner.

ABOUT THE AUTHOR

Bitrus Raphael Medugu is teacher by profession and cleric by calling. Over the years, he has taken a very special interest in self-help tips, and he has been writing lately to contribute to helping people better their lives. He is currently a teacher of Systematic Theology.